Sleep and Dreams

Sleep and Dreams

BY RAE LINDSAY

illustrated by
LEIGH GRANT

Franklin Watts
New York / London / 1978
A First Book

Library of Congress Cataloging in Publication Data

Lindsay, Rae.
    Sleep and dreams.

    (A First book)
    Bibliography: p.
    Includes index.
    SUMMARY: Discusses the stages of sleep, sleep
disorders, dream and sleep research, and cures for
sleeplessness.
        1.   Sleep—Juvenile literature.   2.   Dreams—
Juvenile literature. [1. Sleep. 2. Dreams]
I. Grant, Leigh. II. Title.
BF1071.L57   154.6   78-5519
ISBN 0-531-01493-2

Contents

Chapter Five
SOMETIMES I JUST CAN'T FALL ASLEEP 41

Chapter Six
ANSWERS TO SOME MORE QUESTIONS ABOUT SLEEP 53

FURTHER READING 59

INDEX 61

For Maria, Sandy and Rob:
angels all . . . when they sleep!

Who Needs Sleep and How Much?

Every living creature needs sleep.

When you see fish lying still at the bottom of a tank, they are actually taking a nap. Crabs, clams and lobsters also stop swimming to sleep, and when birds need a rest, they tuck their heads beneath their wings. The largest land animal of all, the slow-moving, lazy-seeming elephant, sleeps about two and a half hours, standing up, every night, even with all the noise of a booming circus around him. In contrast, the sleek tiger, who seems so active, sleeps about sixteen hours a day.

Babies sleep most of the time, while elderly people appear to need less sleep, and possibly, your parents complain about never getting *enough* sleep. "If I could just stay in bed for one more hour. . . ." On an average, though, most of us sleep about seven to eight hours a day . . . a little more if you're under twenty, a little less if you're over sixty. Basically we spend one-third of our lives sleeping.

YOUR BODY KNOWS
WHAT TIME IT IS

The amount we sleep has very little to do with whether it's dark or light outside. Where Eskimos live, it's dark almost twenty-four hours a day during the winter. But they still don't get much more than eight hours of sleep.

Sleep is really under the control of a body clock or clocks which produce what scientists call "circadian rhythms." *Circa* means "about" and *dian* means "a day." In other words, many of our life's rhythms operate on a twenty-four-hour-a-day cycle: eight hours to sleep and sixteen hours for wide-awake activities.

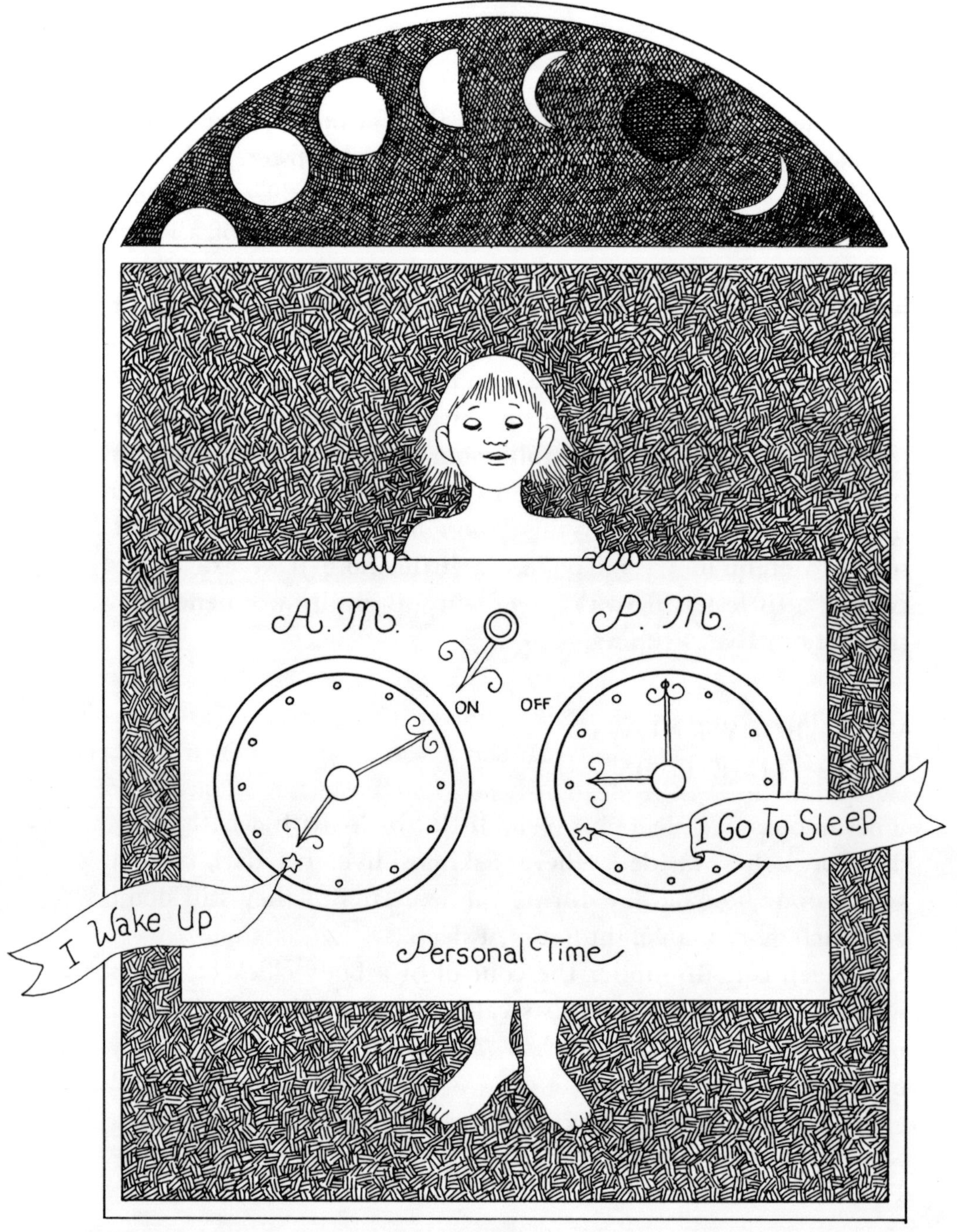

A. M.
P. M.
ON
OFF
I Wake Up
I Go To Sleep
Personal Time

The theory of circadian rhythms has been proven by researchers who have gone into dark caves for weeks at a time. Here, where there is no "daytime" or "nighttime" as we know it, most people adopt roughly the same twenty-four-hour cycles, give or take a few minutes. They sleep about eight hours and are awake about sixteen—without alarm clocks or sunlight and nightfall to tell them when to sleep and when to wake up.

Further evidence of this rhythm occurs with pilots or people who travel long distances. If you fly to London from New York, when you arrive it will be five hours later than New York time. At 12 midnight in London, you probably won't be ready for bed because it is actually only 7:00 P.M. in New York. In the morning, you may wake up at noon in London because it is really 7:00 A.M. according to your normal, New York "body time." Several days will go by before you adjust to the time change. This is called "jet lag."

The former American Secretary of State, Henry Kissinger, who flew millions of miles all over the globe, never seemed bothered by jet lag. Since he had a bed on his plane, whenever possible, he went to sleep at his *regular* Eastern Standard Time, even though it might be 11:00 A.M. in the part of the world he was visiting.

Pilots, of course, are not always able to sleep when they want to or need to. Although they have trained themselves to deal with a certain amount of jet lag, this becomes a greater problem on longer trips—let's say from Chicago to Australia or Hong Kong. When the time difference is as much as seven or eight hours, a pilot may have to rest for a day or so, because when a person has been deprived of regular sleep for an extended period he or she becomes irritable, accident-prone and not as capable at performing his or her job.

This common problem of transcontinental pilots illustrates the need every human being has for a certain amount of sleep every day. But although there is no question about the need for sleep, it is not so easy to understand *why* we need to sleep.

WHY IS SLEEP NECESSARY?

For thousands of years people have been fascinated by the sleep habits of human beings and animals. In ancient times people believed sleep freed the soul so it could enter the spirit world. Aristotle, a famous Greek philosopher and scientist of the fourth century B.C., noticed that people often fell asleep after eating a big meal. He decided that digestion brings on sleep. As proof, he pointed out that babies always fall asleep after a meal. Babies *do* fall asleep after eating, but the cause of sleep is not digestion itself.

Another theory proposed for centuries is that we sleep because we're *tired*. But if that were so, people who have physical jobs, such as a football player or a miner who work mainly with their bodies, would require more sleep than a computer operator or a writer, whose work demands more brainpower than muscle. In truth, the football player, the miner, the computer operator and the writer all need just about the same average of seven hours and twenty minutes of sleep per night.

Today's sleep researchers are still searching for the answer to why we must sleep. No experiment has ever been able to prove that there is a basic difference between actual sleeping or simply closing your eyes and resting (aside from the fact that when we are asleep, we dream). Although there are several theories, actually there are only two schools of thought about the need for sleep. One group of researchers believes that when we sleep brain tissue and other body cells are recharged (similar to the way you charge a battery).

Another group of scientists is convinced that our need for sleep has been programmed into us genetically from the time of earliest man as a way of surviving. For example, instead of sleeping at night, if the early cavemen had hunted for food or water, the hunt would have been perilous because of the lack of light. They might then have become the prey of animals who are programmed or adapted for night hunting. In other words, staying up during the night simply wasn't safe.

Despite the theories, scientists would have to agree with what we all know to be true: we feel much better when we've had a good night's sleep. Our bodies are telling us we *need* that sleep.

In the last twenty-five years researchers have come up with some other possible answers to the mystery of sleep. Their experiments show that there are parts of the brain which regulate the body chemistry, sending signals telling us to sleep for a certain amount of time every day. The signals are sent from the brain stem, an area about the size of your little finger, which connects the spinal cord with the brain and controls many functions such as eye movements, swallowing, breathing, heart rate, as well as wakefulness.

Signals tell you when to go to sleep and when to wake up. The system is controlled by chemical "messengers" called *hormones*. While the body manufactures these messengers automatically, science is finding ways to inject such chemicals artificially to help people who have trouble either sleeping or staying awake.

Sometimes when the brain is injured, the sleep unit no longer gets the messages and the person suffers from diseases such as "sleeping sickness" or a state resembling long, uninterrupted sleeping called "coma." Coma actually means a "state of prolonged unconsciousness due to disease, injury or poison," and is from the Greek word *koma,* meaning "deep sleep." A coma may last a few days, months or even years. One well-known case is Karen Ann Quinlan, who took a combination of sleeping pills and alcohol which damaged her brain, and has been in a coma for more than two years.

But there are other examples where sleeping for long periods of time is not caused by a coma at all. For instance, some mammals sleep or rest all winter long. They are "hibernating." Before winter, squirrels, raccoons, possums, even bears, stock up on food by eating furiously for weeks. Then they retire to a cave or nest in the ground to hibernate through the winter. They emerge in the spring much thinner and very, very hungry. The reason these animals can live in a sleeplike state all during the winter is that their body temperatures drop about 60° F (15° C), almost to freezing, and their heartbeat and breathing rates are drastically reduced so that they need very little food.

NAPS COUNT, TOO

Although human beings on an average spend a third of each day sleeping, you don't have to get *all* your required sleep at one time. Babies don't, for example. They rest several times during the day. Animals spend as much as two-thirds of their lives sleeping or resting. Rats take ten naps a day; rabbits take sixteen to twenty-one rests; worms rest four times every day; and cats are always falling off to sleep—that's where we get the expression "catnap." In fact, cats sleep a total of about seventeen hours a day.

Many famous people who lead busy lives acquire the habit of taking regular naps throughout the day. Thomas Edison, for example, only slept two hours a night, but he rested for two or three hours during the day, and at the museum named after him in Edison, New Jersey, an important part of his office is the narrow bed where he took his "forty winks." Sir Winston Churchill always took a nap in the early afternoon, and so did the American Presidents Truman, Kennedy, and Johnson.

Sleep researchers have noticed that modern people sleep less than men and women of earlier times, or even those who live in existing primitive situations—remote islands, or far-off mountains, or other places that have not been changed by "civilization." According to one British expert on sleep, Dr. Mangalore Pai, people stay awake longer today because there is much more to keep them busy during the nighttime hours. In more simple societies the natives sleep about ten or eleven hours a day. But in more sophisticated societies people can go to see a film, watch television, or go for a drive. These are all activities that stimulate our brains and our bodies.

But no matter how many times you stay up late to watch television or enjoy a party, eventually you will fall asleep for your normal amount of time. If you need ten hours of sleep a night and only get seven, tomorrow you will be tired and will probably go to bed early to make up for the loss. You will be falling into that twenty-four-hour-a-day cycle we talked about.

As far as we know, there are only three men in the whole world who *never* need sleep at all: one is an Italian farmer, the second is an Australian and the third is a Spaniard who claims he lost all desire to sleep in 1904 and has not slept since. Their cases have been closely studied but there is no scientific explanation offered for their ability to stay awake all the time. Apart from them, the record for staying awake is just under twelve days. It was set in 1968 by Mrs. Bertha Van Der Merwe, a Capetown, South Africa, housewife, who went without sleep for 282 hours and 55 minutes (11 days, 18 hours and 55 minutes). The rest of us should have regular sleep—every single night—to feel at our best.

Chapter Two

What Happens to Me When I Sleep?

Do you know that expression, "I slept like a log?" It's inaccurate because *nobody* sleeps like a log . . . except a log. Even though you may think that you sleep in the same position all night long, most of us change our positions about thirty times a night. Some psychologists believe that the way we sleep reveals something about how we feel during our waking hours.

Basically, there are six different ways to sleep, and although we may like one best, throughout the night we vary our posture.

The different sleep postures and what they reveal, described below, were discovered as part of the continuing research being done to find out what happens when we sleep.

1. PRONE: You sleep sprawled out on your stomach, a way of announcing that you have taken over the entire territory of your bed.

2. MUMMY: You wrap yourself up totally in the covers, even your head, as a way of "escaping" from the world.

3. SEMI-FETAL: A return to the posture you had in your mother's womb before you were born. Your head rests on one arm and your legs are bent slightly. People who sleep in this position are often tense, afraid to relax completely, to let go, but this also shows they are sensible and well-balanced.

4. THE BOXER: On your back with your legs straight out and your arms clutching the covers as if they are an enemy.

5. THE SPOON: Married couples often sleep like this, resembling the way two spoons look when stacked together.

6.   THE ROYAL: You are stretched out on your back, arms stretched out on either side and legs flung out. You feel like a king or queen and are happy with your daytime world.

HOW SLEEP RESEARCH IS DONE

Although man has been observing the mysteries of sleep for thousands of years, it is only in the last thirty years that scientists have had some dramatic breakthroughs.

The most important discoveries were made possible by the use of a "polygraph," an instrument that measures bodily functions. The most revealing variation of this device is the "electroencephalograph." (*Electro* measures electricity, *encephalo* is the Greek word for "brain," and *graph* means a "written record.") The nickname for this instrument is an EEG. EEGs were first used in other areas of medicine in 1929, but it was only in the late forties and early fifties that the device was used to study sleep.

At that time doctors and scientists were beginning to specialize in research at special "sleep laboratories." At sleep labs, people who sleep normally, as well as those who have trouble sleeping, are studied with the help of EEGs while they sleep or try to sleep. If you are a patient at a sleep lab, you get ready for bed in a room that resembles an ordinary hotel room; then wires (electrodes) are taped to your head—this doesn't hurt at all—some near the eyes to record eye movements, others near the forehead, the sides of the head and near the ears.

While you sleep, the wires carry the messages from your brain to the EEG which in turn reports the movements as lines on a roll of paper. In fact, on a normal night, from a thousand to fifteen hundred feet of paper will be used to record your brain waves. The wires also tell scientists about other changes in your sleeping body: eye movements are measured, muscle activity is recorded and heart activity is registered.

THE STAGES OF SLEEP

If you were a researcher in a sleep lab, you would notice that, normally, patients go through four different stages of sleep, all indicated by the EEG markings. Sleep isn't simply a quiet resting time, interrupted by dreams that come now and then. Sleep follows a definite pattern:

☆STAGE ONE: You just begin to drift off to sleep. The brain waves on an EEG are small and fast, quite different from the waves which are recorded when we are awake. The body muscles start to relax, the temperature drops steadily and the heart beats more slowly. At this stage you change positions often.

☆STAGE TWO: On an EEG, the waves become slower, with some faster waves called "sleep spindles" every now and then for the next thirty minutes or so. You may still be trying to find the most comfortable position.

☆STAGE THREE: About forty-five minutes after you go to sleep, you enter "deep sleep," the period in which the blood pressure has dropped and the EEG line is more even, with larger, slower, more regular waves. You are not so easily awakened at this stage.

☆STAGE FOUR: The deepest sleep—the brain waves are slow, large, regular. The body goes through very few movements and it is difficult to wake someone up during Stage Four; sometimes only a very loud noise will do it. Stage Four is the time when some people talk in their sleep or sleepwalk.

After a few minutes in Stage Four, the sleeper starts working his or her way back through the stages of sleep: a few minutes in Stage Three, still very sound sleep; back to the lighter sleep of Stage Two; and then, at the point that would have been Stage One sleep, the sleeper begins to dream. About ninety minutes have gone by. The dreaming stage will take about twenty minutes before the sleeper drifts back into Stage Two and continues the down-again, up-again pattern. (The entire pattern is repeated four to six times a night.)

As the night goes on, the dreaming periods become longer and the deep sleeping stages are shorter. Toward morning, dreams may last more than an hour.

We know all about this now, but just twenty-five years ago the understanding that there were different types of sleep—dreaming sleep and nondreaming sleep—came about quite by accident.

In 1952, a very distinguished sleep researcher, Dr. Nathaniel Kleitman, was working at the University of Chicago. Dr. Kleitman was curious about the way the eyes moved during sleep, and he assigned his researchers to follow through on this study. A young graduate student, Eugene Aserinsky, noticed that in addition to the slow, rolling movements of the eyes during sleep, at some times during the night, the eyes darted around energetically, just as if the person were awake.

(If you wonder how you can tell what a person's eyes are doing when they are closed, try this simple experiment with a

TENSE
MUSCLE
RELAX
HIGH
TEMPERATURE
LOW
FAST
HEART
SLOW

HIGH
LOW
BLOOD PRESSURE
SELECT ONE
QUIET SLEEP
SNORE
TALK
SLEEPWALK

friend. Ask him or her to close his or her eyes and move them; then see if you can tell which way they're moving.)

At the Chicago sleep lab, of course, they were using a machine to record eye movements in addition to visual observation. The researchers began to see a relation between eye movements and sleep stages. In fact, the eyes only moved *rapidly* during the dream stages of sleep. According to Dr. William C. Dement, now a famous expert on sleep at Stanford University in California, but at that time a medical student in his second year at Chicago, "This was *the* breakthrough—the discovery that changed the course of sleep research."

For now they realized there was a real difference between dreaming and nondreaming sleep. Dr. Dement coined the term REM for "rapid eye movement" sleep, the "active sleep which only occurs when people are dreaming." "Quiet" sleep is known as NREM (non-REM) sleep in which the eyes are moving very slowly and the body is fairly relaxed, although the person may actually be moving his or her body all night long.

During REM sleep, when you do most of your dreaming, the brain waves resemble the waves of waking life, even though breathing is irregular and the heart rate increases and the large muscles of the arms, legs and torso are limp. In boys the penis becomes erect (this has nothing to do with the content of their dreams). While the brain and eyes are active and the brain waves are closest to an *awake* stage, the rest of the body is very relaxed. For this reason REM sleep has also been called "paradoxical sleep." (A *paradox* is a situation that seems to be contradictory but is nonetheless true.)

Although researchers still haven't discovered exactly *why* we sleep, the discovery of REM sleep opened up exciting possibilities for the study of dreams and their meaning.

Chapter Three

Do Birds Dream, Too?

Birds may not dream, but cats, dogs, human beings and all other mammals do dream—every time they fall asleep. Because dreaming is a universal human experience, people have wondered about the meaning of dreams for centuries.

Four thousand years ago, the Egyptians thought dreaming was so important they built temples to Serapis, the god of dreams, with the hope of inspiring happy or helpful dreams. They also had "dream books" which interpreted the meaning of dreams. Such books were still popular during the time of ancient Greece, the Roman Empire and until recent times. The Bible has more than seventy passages about dreams and their significance.

In some primitive societies, natives believe that dreams foretell the future. Another theory is that during sleep your soul goes away for a while so that it can act out whatever events you have been dreaming about.

But it was only at the beginning of our century that individual meaning was attached to dreams. Dr. Sigmund Freud, who is often called "The Father of Psychiatry," felt that what we dream is related to our own hopes and goals and fears. In his book, *The Interpretation of Dreams* (published in 1900), he wrote that dreams are "the guardians of sleep," which protect us from things that might bother us.

Freud believed our dreams were very personal. Images and events in dreams mean different things to different people. For example, a frog may represent a happy outing at a lake to one person, but may simply stand for an unpleasant creature to another.

Some researchers think that during REM sleep certain things that have happened during the day become part of our permanent memories. As Dr. Peter Hauri, director of the Dartmouth Sleep Laboratory in Hanover, New Hampshire, explains, the function of dreaming is to go over what happened during the day, "especially those things we weren't able to make sense of and those things we couldn't pay attention to." During our dreams we add what we need to our storehouse of memories while throwing out the "rubbish," the things we don't have to retain.

The importance of dreaming is illustrated by what happens to people who are *prevented* from sleeping and therefore dreaming.

The disastrous effects of lack of sleep were well known in the Middle Ages when Europeans were frightened by so-called witches. One way of getting suspects to admit they were witches was to torture them by forcing them to stay awake. In many cases the victims were mentally disturbed to begin with, and the long periods without sleep and dreams made them behave even more strangely, which was then considered proof that they were witches.

In more recent times, the practice of "brainwashing" came about when American prisoners of war were kept awake for days after they were captured by Communists during the Korean War in the 1950s. The prisoners became confused, hysterical, ready to believe and admit to any of the things their captors told them so they could have the blessed relief of sleep.

Fortunately, "sleep deprivation," as this is called, usually doesn't cause permanent damage. For an experiment, a disc jockey, Peter Tripp, stayed awake for 201 hours in a "wake-a-thon" to raise money for charity. Although his behavior became more and more erratic—he was angry, hallucinating (he thought people were trying to hurt him), depressed—when he finally did go to sleep for twelve hours, he had many more REM periods than the normal four to six a night. And it took several months for him to get over his feeling of sadness and depression.

In sleep laboratories, researchers have seen that if patients are awakened every time they drift into REM sleep, they will make up for this loss the following night, getting almost double the amount of dream sleep to catch up. This is what scientists refer to as "REM Rebound," or "Dream Rebound."

People who take sleeping pills or other drugs, or who drink a great deal of alcohol, are usually deprived of REM sleep. When they stop taking the drugs or alcohol, they may have awful nightmares because the amount of REM sleep is so intensified. A person who has had no REM sleep for days or weeks will eventually "explode" with a rapid series of dreams, one right after the other. This is also an example of "REM Rebound."

These extreme examples of what happens when we are deprived of dreaming sleep have led some sleep experts to theorize that the major reason we sleep is to *dream*. It may be that the major function of sleep is to allow the healing, helpful work of dreams to occur.

DREAMS RELATE TO REAL LIFE

Although it may seem that you have the most fantastic, weirdest dreams, most scientists believe that whatever we dream about has to be something we could have *imagined* during waking hours. You can't dream about inventing a computer if you have no engineering knowledge. You *could* dream about punch-

ing buttons to operate a computer, yes, but you would not be able to *design* a computer in your dreams.

We do actively participate in our dreams, however, almost as if we are an audience at a show. Your eyes will follow the action of a dream, and if you're dreaming about a tennis match, your eyes will move from side to side to side just as if you were *really* at a tennis match. Even babies, who can't speak and may not yet be able to see clearly, spend almost half of their sleeping time in rapid eye movement sleep.

People who have been blind since birth have dreams, too, but they do not have REM sleep in the sense of *watching* the dream. A blind person's dreams have no coloration or visual impressions as sighted people's dreams do; his or her dreams are made up of different sense impressions, such as smelling or hearing or feeling.

Most of our dreams occur in situations we know: a third of them happen in a house; one-quarter of them take place in moving vehicles—buses, cars, planes, boats, trains.

We don't always recognize the people in our dreams. In fact, 40 percent of the time we're dreaming about strangers. In one out of four dreams, all we're doing is watching the action of others in the dream—we are bystanders, not really able to control what is happening. These are the cases when, if the dream becomes too horrifying, we often wake up because we can't actively change what's going on in the dream.

Some dreams are described as "wish fulfillment," a term chosen by Dr. Freud. This means your dreams try to provide the kind of happiness that perhaps you can't have in real life. If you're lonely or want to be with a certain friend or pet, you may find yourself making that person or animal a key part of your dreams. This is true, too, if you've lost someone you loved—if he or she has moved away, or has been sick or died. Wish-fulfillment dreams are more likely with children than with adults; frequently adults have more complicated dreams which seem to be "censored" or "edited," perhaps to protect them from problems they are really worried about.

It's a good idea to talk to your parents or your brothers or sisters about your dreams. In some societies, discussing the night's dreams is a regular routine. The Senoi tribesmen, who live in the equatorial rain forest of the Malay Peninsula, don't know how to read or write, but it's part of their culture for the children to talk about their dreams over breakfast every day. The Senoi people are very happy and tranquil. They are satisfied with their lives, and many anthropologists who study primitive societies often point to the Senoi as a well-adjusted, successful cultural group. Perhaps we could take a tip from them and try to talk about our dreams with our family, or even write about our dreams for a class assignment.

PROBLEM SOLVING
IN DREAMS

Sometimes a dream can provide the answer to an actual problem you couldn't solve during waking hours. Dr. Dement, who has done so much research on sleep, reported that although he smoked two packs of cigarettes a day, he was never able to break the habit. Finally one night he had a vivid dream that he had lung cancer. In his dream he saw the X rays of his lungs and knew he would never see his family grow up or do all the work he wanted to do. When he woke up, he says, "I felt I was reborn." He stopped smoking immediately.

Other kinds of problem solving are possible while dreaming. Mathematicians have been known to solve complicated calculus problems while dreaming, even though the solutions eluded them during the day. The famous golfer, Jack Nicklaus, told a reporter for the *San Francisco Chronicle* that he couldn't understand why his golfing scores were down until he dreamed he was holding the golf club in a slightly different way from his normal grip. The next day he swung the club as he had in his dream and his scores quickly improved.

There have also been accounts of creative activities that occur during dreams. Robert Louis Stevenson reported that his dreams gave him the plots for many of his famous stories, including *Doctor Jekyll and Mr. Hyde*. Comedian-songwriter Steve Allen woke up from a dream with the music for "This Could Be the Start of Something Big," his bestselling song. Unfortunately, if a person is not awakened soon after such a dream or doesn't immediately record the inspiration, he or she may forget exactly what was solved or created. Samuel Taylor Coleridge said that he composed several hundred lines of his poem, "Kubla Khan," during a dream. Although he woke up immediately afterward, a friend interrupted his work, and when he tried to remember his dream an hour later, he could only recall about ten lines.

For a time it was popular for people to listen to tapes while they were sleeping to learn a foreign language or study for an exam, but no definite proof exists to show this is really effective. In fact, most research about sleep learning shows it is only possible during the lightest Stage One sleep, but not during the deeper stages. It appears that the insights we may gain during REM or dreaming sleep cannot be programmed, but happen on their own.

Chapter Four

Why Do We Walk, Talk,
Snore in Our Sleep?

Since we do spend one-third of our lives asleep, it would be convenient if, while sleeping, everything went along smoothly. But we already know that dreams can sometimes be unpleasant as well as pleasant. In addition, there are problems quite different from those that pop up in the dreaming stage. These are called "sleep disorders."

One kind of disorder is the need for too much sleep, called "hypersomnia." Another is "insomnia" which is not being able to get enough sleep. And a third is a group of disorders which includes night terrors, sleepwalking, sleeptalking and bed-wetting. Another problem that may occur when we sleep is snoring.

Several of these disorders happen during Stage Four sleep. In this deepest stage of sleep, the mind lets down all its fences, and things that have been troubling you emotionally come out. But persons who walk, talk or even scream in their sleep usually have no memory of what has happened when they wake up. Most children outgrow these problems before they become teenagers. In addition to mental causes, some sleep disorders happen because of physical reasons that are inherited.

SLEEPWALKING—
IT RUNS IN THE FAMILY

A million Americans are sleepwalkers. Usually sleepwalking has nothing to do with dreaming. Remember, in the REM stage of sleep, your arms and legs cannot move even though your eyes are doing an active job observing your dreams. Sleepwalking actually occurs during Stage Four, non-REM sleep.

The fact that sleepwalking is inherited has been proven in hundreds of cases. One of the strangest involved a family in

which all four members walked in their sleep. One night, they all met at the kitchen table to have what they thought was Christmas dinner. Although none of the somnambulists—the sleepwalkers—remembered their nocturnal adventures the next day, a visitor who was awakened by all this activity was able to report the strange dinner "party" to sleep researchers. After all, he had celebrated Christmas with them—even though it was only September.

NOW'S THE TIME
FOR A LITTLE TALK

Have you ever tried to sleep with someone who talks in his or her sleep? It's eerie because the sleeper will carry on an entire complicated conversation with some known or unknown person, sounding very sensible and reasonable all the time. Although you are able to eavesdrop during the talk, again, the next day, the sleeptalker won't remember any of his or her remarks at all. Talking in one's sleep usually takes place when someone is happy (or troubled) about events of the day, but like sleepwalking, it has nothing to do with dreaming.

NOCTURNAL ACCIDENTS

Bed-wetting (called "enuresis") is very distressing even if it happens only occasionally. And it doesn't occur only with children: at least 2 percent of adults suffer from nighttime accidents. These mishaps seem to be caused by being in such a deep stage of sleep that the signal to go to the bathroom doesn't get through to the brain.

If your parents are concerned about this problem with you, they might try waking you up for a trip to the bathroom around midnight, before they go to bed. It also helps not to drink water or any other liquids before bedtime.

But enuresis is something most of us grow out of as our body systems become more mature and we learn to control and predict what's happening. Most adults, for example, will automatically wake up *before* an accident occurs.

SLEEPING SICKNESS— A MYSTERIOUS DISEASE

Sleeping sickness, or narcolepsy, is a rare disease that causes people to fall asleep at the oddest times during the day. In the middle of a conversation, or while playing football, or when they're trying to make chocolate cake, for example. Someone once fell asleep in twenty feet of water, while scuba diving. Fortunately, he was not diving alone and his companion got him up to the surface quickly. Another narcoleptic often falls asleep when he is introduced to someone; this is embarrassing because not only is he a successful businessman, but he is married to a prominent political figure.

Narcolepsy affects as many as a hundred thousand people in the United States. The number is probably even higher, but many people who suffer from sleeping sickness have not had the proper diagnosis of their problem. (Since they fall asleep so often, people are inclined to think of them as "lazy" or even somewhat mentally retarded.)

But studies have shown that narcoleptics begin the night *not* with non-REM, Stage One sleep, but with *REM* sleep (dreaming sleep). They go immediately from an awake stage into a dreaming stage where their large muscles are limp. With narcoleptics, this same paralysis also takes over *anytime*—unpredictably—during the day. Unfortunately, there is no way of guessing when this daytime, REM-type sleep will take place.

One of the ongoing projects of researchers at all sleep labs is to try to find a cure for narcolepsy. Before they can, though, they have to find out what causes this strange illness. In the meantime, doctors can deal with the problem by prescribing certain drugs which keep the patient awake all during the day.

THE STORY OF SNORING

There have been hundreds of funny jokes made about snoring, but it's no laughing matter for the people who live with someone who snores every night. Snoring is really a form of noisy breathing that happens when a person sleeps with his or her mouth open. There are hundreds of millions of adults throughout the world who suffer from this problem.

Sleeping on your back will encourage snoring. In some cases, nose and throat problems or air pollution are the triggers that bring on the disturbing noises. It's less common for children to snore, and when they do it's often because they have swollen tonsils or adenoids or are suffering with a bad cold.

Snorers are in very good company. Many, many American presidents have been notorious snorers, including George Washington, Lincoln, Andrew Johnson, Teddy Roosevelt, Taft, Harding, Hoover and Franklin D. Roosevelt. We have no historic records to date as to whether Truman, Eisenhower, Ken-

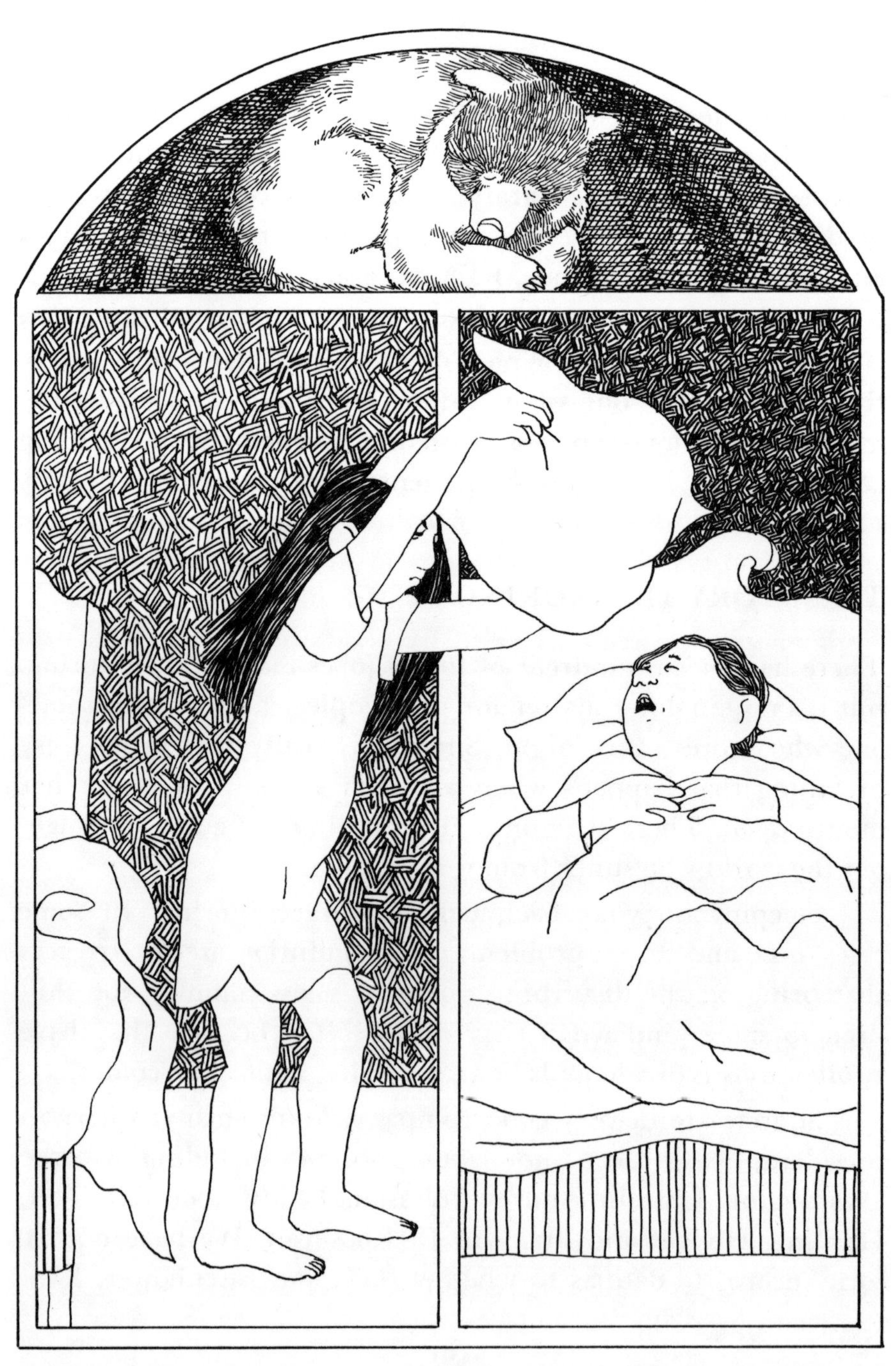

nedy, Lyndon Johnson, Nixon, Ford or Jimmy Carter, were or are snorers.

Because snoring is so annoying to anyone trying to sleep in the same room, many preventive or corrective inventions have been designed to beat snoring. In 1918, an E. V. Galiardo invented a muzzle-type gadget that fit over the chin and mouth, forcing snorers to breathe through their noses. Another device looks much like the bit you place in a horse's mouth.

The Chinese believe that using a wooden pillow will prevent snoring. Another old-fashioned remedy was to wear a harness that would keep the snorer from turning onto his back, the position most common for snoring. (You are less likely to snore if you lie on your side.) It's no surprise that all of these inventions or solutions were devised by people who were disturbed night after night by those who snored!

It's also interesting that American Indians are said never to snore—nor do they stutter. The reason, according to a former teacher at an Indian reservation, is that Indian children are taught to sleep with their mouths *closed,* so they won't get diseases or illnesses of the throat.

ANOTHER KIND OF SNORING

"Sleep apnea" is the name for another breathing problem that happens to adults during sleep. Those who have sleep apnea actually stop breathing while they sleep and must wake up in order to breathe. Such patients observed at sleep labs fall asleep and stop breathing for 20 to 135 seconds. Then they wake up with a very loud snoring sound and take huge gasps of air to fill their lungs; they fall asleep again and repeat this pattern hundreds of times all night long.

People who have sleep apnea aren't aware of the fact that they really can't sleep *and* breathe at the same time. And their husbands or wives usually think they are snoring when in fact they are actually gasping for air.

Researchers are studying the use of several drugs to help treat apnea, but up to now there isn't any one drug treatment that works. In some extreme cases, doctors perform an operation in which a patient is able to breathe while asleep through the use of a tube inserted into a hole in the throat.

As with snoring, many times more men than women are likely to suffer from apnea, and the problem gets worse as people get older. Another mysterious fact about apnea is that it strikes people who don't get enough sleep (insomniacs) as well as those who complain of needing *too* much sleep (hypersomniacs).

Chapter Five

Sometimes I Just Can't Fall Asleep

There are some lucky people or children who can fall asleep easily no matter what has happened during the day. For most of us, though, such things as hunger, anxiety, too much exercise, not enough exercise, too much happiness or excitement can keep us awake for hours.

This occasional sleeplessness is very different from chronic insomnia—the serious inability to sleep that recurs night after night.

People who always fall asleep in ten or fifteen minutes can be called "good sleepers"; poor sleepers take from thirty to fifty minutes to fall asleep and often wake up during the night. If you're a very light sleeper who is easily awakened, or you find you toss and turn for what seems hours before you finally drift into sleep, here are some things to help ensure a good night's rest:

THE RIGHT MATTRESS

Egyptians invented the mattress four thousand years ago. The earliest version was simply a pad stuffed with wool or feathers which could be rolled up for easy storage—in fact, it looked very much like a sleeping bag.

Later on, during the Middle Ages, the great French king, Charlemagne, had his mattress placed on a wooden platform. He may have done this to put some distance between himself and the insects and rodents that crawled around in his field tent while he was fighting his many famous battles. Even though the rigid platform and the thin mattress must have made King Charlemagne feel as if he were sleeping in the street, this was really the forerunner of our modern beds.

Although it's fun to rough it in a camp bed or in a sleeping bag now and then, you wouldn't be too happy sleeping this way every night. You sleep best in a comfortable bed with a good, thick mattress, which should be firm enough to support your back. Usually, a mattress is placed on top of springs to give your body some flexibility, unlike Charlemagne's wooden, unyielding platform. If your mattress is too soft it will be difficult to find a satisfying position.

Sometimes, a mattress gets worn in one spot from your sleeping in the same place every night. It may be that all you have to do is turn the mattress over to uncover a new and comfortable cushion for your bed.

HOW MANY PILLOWS?

Some people like very soft pillows made of goose or duck feathers called "down"; others like firmer pillows made of foam rubber. If you find that you sneeze a lot you may be allergic to the feather stuffing and should ask your mother for a substitute.

There's no rule to follow about how many pillows are right for you—you may be more comfortable with two pillows or even with none. But if you find that your pillow becomes a punching bag—that you're either flattening it out or plumping it up, experiment with more or fewer until you get the right balance.

THE COVER-UP

Even though the indoor temperature may be around 70° F (20° C) all year long, during the winter extra blankets seem to help you fall asleep faster and certainly feel snug. When you do have an extra blanket or quilt on your bed, you may find you're quite comfortable with a room temperature of 60° to 65° F (15.5° to 18.3° C), which would really make United States President Carter happy, since he emphasizes energy conservation so much.

In summertime, the opposite may be true, although once again, this is a matter for personal preference. In one family I know, the daughter can't sleep unless she's bundled up in a puffy quilt, summer or winter; her brother, in the very next room, chooses only the lightest blanket, and more often than not, kicks off even that during the night.

Remember, your body temperature drops during the night, so although it may seem very warm when you go to bed, toward dawn you will probably snuggle up in your covers to make up for the temperature change.

LET IN SOME AIR

No matter how many blankets you choose, you should always sleep with a window open at least a crack to let in some fresh air. It's not only good for you, but helps you to fall asleep. Even the sound of the wind or the rain can make you sleepy, while a stuffy room, filled with stale air, can keep you awake.

BEDTIME SNACKS

When you were little you probably used the excuse of a glass of milk or just one more piece of cake as a way of stalling for time before bed.

Actually, though, a bedtime snack can help you to fall asleep for several reasons. It's difficult to sleep when you're hungry, so some milk and cake eliminate this problem.

But more important, milk contains a chemical (tryptophane) that acts like a natural sleeping pill. (The presence of tryptophane in a baby's milk is what encourages sleep.) Malt-based drinks such as Ovaltine, or yogurt and honey also have this special chemical and will probably help you to fall asleep.

One nice nighttime special is a cup of warm milk to which you add a sprinkle of cinnamon and one teaspoon of honey—good for you nutritionally, too!

OTHER SLEEP INDUCERS

While you have a nighttime snack, it's pleasant to read a happy book—not an adventure story—to put you in a restful mood before lights-out time. A warm bath is also a soothing solution.

If you have trouble sleeping, there are new records and tapes specifically meant to lull you to sleep. One special device is called a "white sound machine," and it reproduces the sound of rain and surf; another company has a series of records of traditional and time-proven sleep inducers, including the sounds of the sea, or thunderstorms, or crickets, or rain in a forest.

Or, you may simply enjoy falling asleep to some mellow, tranquil music, but probably not The Who or the Rolling Stones.

Above all, if you have a problem on your mind—if you're worried about a test at school, or you've had a fight with your best friend—try to talk this out before bedtime with your parents or a brother or sister. It's very difficult to fall asleep at night when you're unhappy or troubled, and it's better to clear the air by talking about it than to toss and turn trying to fall asleep.

Remember, too, that a regular routine before bedtime will help you to fall asleep more easily. It also helps a great deal if you go to bed—and wake up—at around the same time each day.

If you follow the suggestions in this book, and still have persistent problems sleeping, it would probably be wise to seek medical attention. It is almost never a good idea to treat yourself by taking any of the over-the-counter sleep aids that are available at drugstores. It is not normal to have serious sleeping problems, especially at this time of your life. If your parents have given you sleep aids or other pills, you might point out that they could be covering up a real medical problem.

WHY DO I HATE TO
GET UP IN THE MORNING?

Just as it's difficult to fall asleep sometimes, everybody has mornings when they hate to get up, when the prospect of doing nothing else but sleeping all day long sounds like the best idea in the world.

Sometimes you feel like this because you went to bed too late the night before and really need more sleep.

Or, you may feel sick and should stay in bed all day.

Sometimes you feel this way because you don't like what lies ahead for the rest of the day: a difficult test at school . . . a crucial soccer game . . . a visit to a relative you don't like at all.

Occasionally you don't want to wake up because you are having a very pleasant dream and it would be great to stay in that dream world for hours.

And some people *always* hate to get up in the morning because they are "night owls": people who are happier going to bed late and sleeping late. You remember in Chapter One we talked about "circadian rhythms," the cycle of twenty-four hours or so which all of us follow? The problem with "circadian rhythms" is that not all these cycles occur during the *same* twenty-four-hour schedule.

Although 90 percent of us could be called "day people" or "larks," who are usually quite happy getting up early in the morning and going to bed reasonably early most nights, 10 percent are "night people" who function best when the rest of the world is sleeping, and like to sleep when everyone else is awake.

This works out fine for those who can arrange their life-style to suit their circadian patterns: for people who work the night shift in factories or hospitals; for entertainers who enjoy staying up all night, every night; for truck drivers who don't mind driving all night on long hauls; for writers or artists or musicians who don't have to go to a regular, nine-to-five job the following day and can stay up all night writing or painting or composing.

Unfortunately, most night owls *must* follow the schedule set by the majority of the population. If you are a night person in school, you must get up and go to your class each morning; there is no nighttime grammar school and even if there were, it would be very lonely with only 10 percent of your classmates. I am a night owl, but I *must* wake up early to get my three children off to school on time, even though I definitely hate to get up in the morning.

Although it is very frustrating to be a night person in a day world, there are ways of adjusting so that you can function more or less smoothly until about noon (a popular start-the-day time for owls). For one thing you should get into the habit

of trying to go to sleep earlier, using some of the ways we talked about earlier. In this way you won't be as tired physically when you do have to get up bright and early in the morning.

Try to give yourself enough time when you wake up so that you don't have to bound out of bed and get going immediately. (This is important for everybody, incidentally. When you've been asleep all night, it's very hard on your body to spring into action suddenly. Just as people don't start cars and immediately drive off at 80 miles (129 km) per hour—they warm them up and build up the speed gradually—you should warm up your body a bit before running it at full speed.)

After the alarm goes off, stretch your arms, then your legs, then your entire body. If you ever watched the way a cat or dog wakes up, you'll realize that they are warming up in the same way.

Make your early-morning time as painless as possible. It's easier if you lay out your clothes the night before, so you don't have to make early-morning decisions. It's better to pack your schoolbooks before you go to bed, so you won't have to scramble around looking for them in the morning. It's a good idea to put out the rubbish the night before to avoid that odious chore in the morning. And it's better to make an arrangement with your brother to walk the dog last thing at night than it is to have to walk it in the morning.

Any of these solutions may not make you much happier about getting up early every morning . . . but it will make life happier for those around you who have to live with you. Unhappily, night people are often grumpy when they have to wake up early, and they can make it miserable for the larks who wake up with a smile on their faces and good thoughts for the day ahead.

Chapter Six

Answers to Some More Questions About Sleep

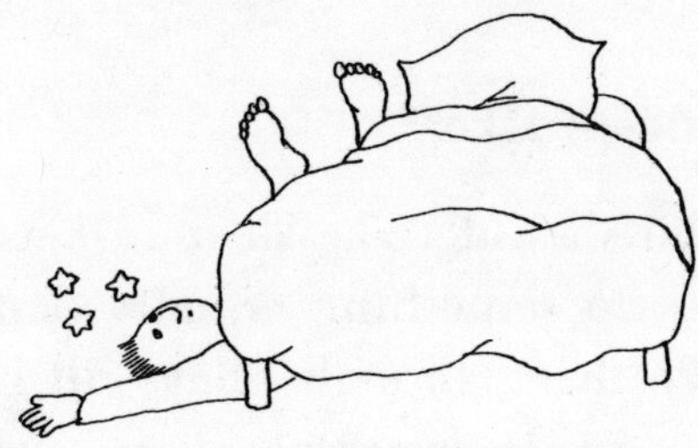

Q. Why do children sometimes fall out of bed?

A. Children fall out of bed when they are in the deepest stages of sleep and so relaxed that they are not in control of their bodies. No one ever falls out of bed in Stage One sleep and rarely during Stage Two sleep when a person is still somewhat aware of the "outside world" and will naturally roll away from the edge of the bed, avoiding that fall.

Q. Who snores more, men or women?

A. Men snore much more than women.

Q. Why does the night go so fast and the day last so long?

A. During your waking hours your brain is active all the time —you are working, playing, studying, eating and participating in your daytime life. At night your brain is resting while you sleep except for the time you're dreaming—and even most dreams are not remembered the following day. So it *seems* as if you've just gone to sleep—and then a few minutes later, it's time to wake up.

Q.   Is it bad to wake a sleepwalker?

A.   No it's not, and you should wake sleepwalkers if they are about to drive a car or do something equally dangerous. Remember, when you wake them, though, they will have no idea whatsoever that they have really been walking in their sleep.

Q.   Is it true that people can fall asleep with their eyes open?

A.   Yes. In sleep experiments subjects have had their eyes taped open, but an EEG will show they are actually asleep, and although their eyes are open, they are not seeing anything. This is because that part of the brain which records sight goes to sleep when you go to sleep.

Q.   Why do you feel sleepy after you've eaten a big meal?

A.   You feel sleepy after Thanksgiving dinner or after eating four doughnuts and two glasses of milk because, in a way, you've taken a sleeping pill. It is the chemical called "tryptophane" (see p. 47) in protein foods like milk, cheese, turkey, other meats and natural sweeteners such as honey or molasses that really does make you sleepy.

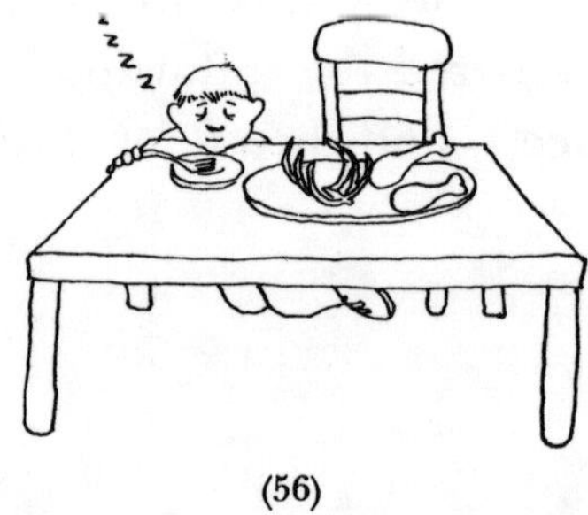

Q. Do you get nightmares from eating
certain foods, like pickles, before bed?

A. No, you don't have nightmares, but when you eat highly spiced or other hard-to-digest food before bed, this prevents you from falling asleep as quickly. You spend more time wide awake, trying to sleep and thinking about how awful you feel. It is possible that when you finally fall asleep and move into a dream stage, that big feast or the four pickles you ate may show up in your dreams, but not necessarily as nightmares.

Q. Why do we yawn when we're sleepy?

A. Before you fall asleep the rate of breathing slows down and you can't get enough oxygen, which causes you to yawn. In the same way, when you're trying to stay awake, yawning gives you more oxygen and fights off sleep temporarily.

Q. Why do I feel tired even when I've slept late?

A. One researcher says, "The longer you sleep, the longer your dreams become. And dreaming is really tiring work in many ways—you wake up feeling almost as if you'd been jogging."

Q.   Who moves around more in their sleep, boys or girls?

A.   Boys are usually more active than girls.

Q.   Do Siamese twins fall asleep at the same time?

A.   No. One of a pair of Siamese twins can fall asleep without the other, and of course, they have quite independent dreams. Think of the problem, though, if one Siamese twin is a sleep-walker and the other isn't!

Q.   How is daydreaming different from real dreaming?

A.   When you daydream, even though you are fantasizing or making up events in your mind, you are actually in control of the dream, as if you are *writing* the story. When you dream at night, it is more as if you are *reading* a story that your brain has written, as if you are an observer who is not in control of what is going to happen.

Q.   Why do people have cold feet when they sleep?

A.   Because the body is lying flat and blood does not circulate as actively to the feet as it does when a person is standing up.

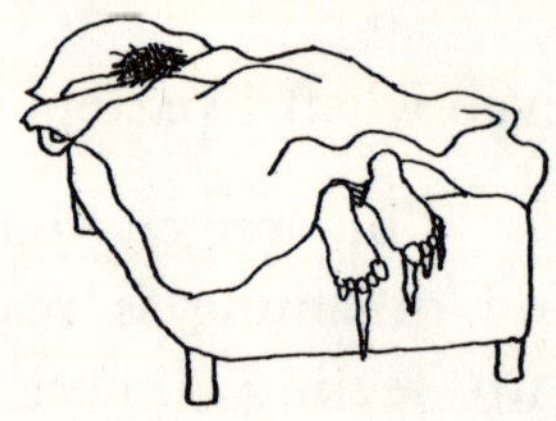

Dunkell, Samuel. *Sleep Positions: The Night Language of the Body*. London: Heinemann, 1977.

Hirsch, Carl S. *Theatre of the Night*. Chicago: Rand McNally, 1976 (adult).

Hoskisson, Jack Bradley. *What is This Thing Called Sleep?* London: Davis-Poynter, 1976.

Kastner, Jonathan, and Kastner, Marianna. *Sleep: The Mysterious Third of Your Life*. New York: Harcourt Brace, 1968 (ages 12 and up).

Kettlekamp, Larry. *Dreams*. New York: Morrow, 1968 (ages 10–14).

Selsam, Millicent. *How Animals Sleep*. New York: Scholastic Book Service, 1969 (ages 5–8).

Silverstein, Alvin, and Silverstein, Virginia. *Sleep and Dreams*. Philadelphia: Lippincott, 1974 (ages 12 and up).

Singer, David L., and Martin, William G. *Sleep on It: A Look at Sleep and Dreams*. Englewood Cliffs, N.J.: Prentice-Hall, 1969 (ages 12 and up).

Smith, Howard E. *Dreams in Your Life*. New York: Doubleday, 1975 (ages 12–14).

Index

RAE LINDSAY
is the author of several books
for adults, and her articles
about lifestyle topics have
appeared widely in magazines.

She lives with her three children
in northern New Jersey, where she
works as a free-lance writer. This is
her first book for young readers.